GRAY

By Patricia M. Stockland
Illustrated by Julia Woolf

Content Consultant
Susan Kesselring, MA
Literacy Educator and K-1 Teacher

magic wagon

(COLORS)

visit us at www.abdopublishing.com

Published by Magic Wagon, a division of the ABDO Publishing Group, 8000 West 78th Street, Edina, Minnesota 55439. Copyright © 2011 by Abdo Consulting Group, Inc. International copyrights reserved in all countries. All rights reserved. No part of this book may be reproduced in any form without written permission from the publisher.

Looking Glass Library™ is a trademark and logo of Magic Wagon.

Printed in the United States of America, North Mankato, Minnesota.
082010
012011

♻ THIS BOOK CONTAINS AT LEAST 10% RECYCLED MATERIALS.

Text by Patricia M. Stockland
Illustrations by Julia Woolf
Edited by Nadia Higgins
Series design by Nicole Brecke
Cover and interior layout by Emily Love

Library of Congress Cataloging-in-Publication Data
Stockland, Patricia M.
  Gray / by Patricia M. Stockland ; illustrated by Julia Woolf.
    p. cm. — (Colors)
  ISBN 978-1-61641-136-7
  1. Gray—Juvenile literature. 2. Colors—Juvenile literature. I. Woolf, Julia. II. Title.
  QC495.5.S7728 2011
  535.6—dc22
                        2010013989

Grandma helps me with my buttons.

My buttons are gray.

4

We walk down the sidewalk.

The sidewalk is gray.

We go to the subway.

The subway car is gray.

We reach the art museum.

The museum is gray.

We see a sculpture.

The sculpture is gray.

Grandma shows me an elephant.

The elephant is gray.

We sit down to have a snack.

The table is gray.

It is raining outside.

The rainy sky is gray.

I buy a bead for Grandma.

The swirls in the bead are gray.

19

Grandma gives me a big hug.

Her soft sweater is gray.

What Is Gray?

There are three primary colors: red, blue, and yellow. These colors combine to make other colors. All three primary colors mixed together make black. Mix white with black, and you make gray.

Primary Colors

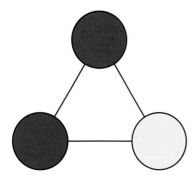

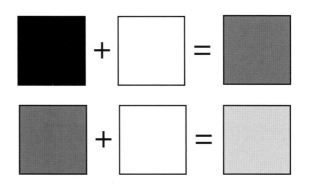

The more white you add, the lighter the gray. How many gray things can you find in this book?

Words to Know

museum—a building where people go to look at beautiful or interesting things.

sculpture—a work of art that is not flat, like a painting, and is usually made of stone, metal, or wood.

subway—a train that goes through tunnels underground.

swirls—looping or twisting bands of color.

Web Sites

To learn more about the color gray, visit ABDO Group online at **www.abdopublishing.com**. Web sites about the colors are featured on our Book Links page. These links are routinely monitored and updated to provide the most current information available.